NUGGETS

OTHER TITLES BY ARTHUR MILTON

Milton on America

How Your Life Insurance Policies Rob You

Life Insurance Stocks: The Modern Gold Rush

How to Get a Dollar's Value for a Dollar Spent

Life Insurance Stocks: An Investment Appraisal

Something More Can Be Done!

Inflation: Everyone's Problem

Insurance Stocks: A Fortune to Share

You Are Worth a Fortune

Will Inflation Destroy America?

A. L. Williams: The Life Insurance Industry's Henry Ford

Tell Yesterday Goodbye!

A Nation Saved: Thank You, President Reagan

Why A. L. Williams Is Right for the Consumer

NUGGETS

Wisdom from Winners

ARTHUR MILTON

BARRICADE BOOKS INC. / NEW YORK

Published by Barricade Books Inc.
150 Fifth Avenue
New York, NY 10011

Printed in the United States of America.

Library of Congress Cataloging-in-Publication Data

Milton, Arthur, 1922–
Nuggets: wisdom from winners / by Arthur Milton.
p. cm.
ISBN 1-56980-114-2
1. Conduct of life—Quotations, maxims, etc.
2. Success—United States—Quotations, maxims, etc.
I. Title.
BJ1611.M56 1997
170'.44—dc21 97–11683
CIP

First printing

DEDICATION

Not to the malcontents, the know-it-alls, the wise guys and gals, the thieves, robbers, murderers of other people's rights and property.

Not to the naysayers nor the motivationally impoverished, nor the lazy, nor the alcoholic or drug addicts, nor to those whose psyches are deranged, nor to horses' asses.

But rather to you, my reader who would not be reading this book if you were not intelligent, capable, motivated, responsible, self-controlled, reasonably happy, reserved, and successful.

TABLE OF CONTENTS

A FEW THOUGHTS FOR THE TWENTY-FIRST CENTURY

Turn the calendar page on a new decade, much less a new century, and prognosticators come out of the woodwork and onto the networks. They have predictions and analyses and near-soothsayings of what is to come. I'm going to join their ranks with a prediction—no, make that a guarantee—of what lies ahead in the twenty-first century. There is no question in my mind that our nation will enjoy its greatest growth and prosperity.

Let the doom-and-gloomers wail otherwise. It's not this magnificent country, but the doomsayers who are doomed. America has worked for and enjoyed great triumphs and fortune since its founding almost

225 years ago. But as a wise philosopher once said, "You ain't seen nothing yet." This will be our greatest of all centuries.

Too many people overlook the basic strengths of the United States. As author John Gunther put it, "Ours is the only country deliberately founded on a good idea." I would take that further. The United States was founded on *many* good ideas, freedoms that allow us to excel. All we need to do is listen to Ralph Waldo Emerson, who urged us to hitch our wagons to a star. It is much easier to do that in the United States than anywhere else on the globe because here the star is so much closer to earth.

There are countless reasons why many of the poor and oppressed (and not so poor and oppressed) of the world want to immigrate to the United States. You don't see Koreans and Pakistanis lining up at the Russian or Chinese embassies for visas. People are clamoring to live here for the protections and the opportunities we offer our citizens—very importantly, the opportunity for financial independence. In 1776, we might have been declaring our independence from England, but we were also issuing a declaration of financial independence when Thomas Jefferson wrote that men are endowed "with certain unalienable rights, that among these are Life, Liberty, and the Pursuit of Happiness."

The right of financial independence is one of our basic freedoms, right up there with freedom of speech, assembly, and religion. It allows for everyone with the grit and gumption to roll up their sleeves, work hard, sweat, and make a good life for themselves and their families. My father, Herman, came to the United States in 1894 at the age of twelve. He worked seven days to take home his $3-per-week pay. But work he did. He never became discouraged because he had the will to succeed.

You see much the same will in our most-recent immigrants, the Koreans. They'll get up at 3 A.M. to be the first ones at the produce market. They'll select the best fruit and vegetables, take it to their store, work for twelve hours, and then start over again the next morning. They want to make it, and they're willing to do whatever they can to reach their goals. A Pace University economist once noted that for a Korean, the store is merely his entry, the first rung on his ladder to success.

There is no fixed sum—$1 million, $10 million, $100 million—when it comes to financial independence. What I mean by that term is whatever it takes for you to not have to rely on anyone else for your needs and wants—not your mother, father, or your government. With planning and initiative—and hard work—you can achieve that independence. It is never too late, or too soon, to chart a financial plan for the rest of your life.

There is a preponderance of choices in this country for those who do work hard, choices ranging from where to go to college to what to eat for breakfast to what to wear to the beach. The American cornucopia exists not only on the Thanksgiving table. It's on display year-round. We have the American free enterprise system to thank for this abundance. It is the American free enterprise system that allows you to plant your personal Fortune Tree. Then it's up to you to water, fertilize, and see that it grows.

Let this book be an antidote to the naysayers who suggest the best was in the past, that the United States will be second-rate and relegated to the rumble seat in the coming years. Let this book be an inspiration to you, the young end of the Baby Boomers, the Generation Xers, babies of the boomers, and those yet to come who will be living in and sculpturing the twenty-first century.

You can learn from those who came before you, whose thoughts and beliefs on patriotism, the work ethic, optimism, and determination are in these pages. You can emulate the success of our most successful and shift into overdrive on the road to financial freedom. There is no reason to look with disdain and suspicion at those who have done well. Figure out what they did, how they did it, and then do it, keeping in mind that there's no need to reinvent the wheel. Never forget, though, that dreams are good as long as you don't grow a wishbone where a backbone should be.

Let me throw in a word of caution here. No matter what you've been told, don't rely too heavily on education. You need practice, not just theory, to go far and do well.

Whatever your goals and dreams, you, the generations of the next century, will have a hard time accomplishing much without a Positive Mental Attitude. I know that every morning I wake up and take my PMA pill. (If only I could bottle it! Move over Bill Gates.) It fills me with optimism and enthusiasm and makes every day better than the last. That's what living is about. Norman Vincent Peale was the great preacher of the power of positive thinking, and he must have done something right. He lived to be ninety-five.

A few years ago, I dedicated another book, *Milton on America*, to my grandchildren, Stephen, Lauren, Pamela, Melissa, Todd, Jennifer, Stephanie, Jonathan, and to all the grandchildren in America. I wrote then, "It is they who will carry our country's torch of freedom into the twenty-first century. It is they who will participate in the great growth and prosperity in the U.S.A. It is they who will benefit from the efforts of their forebears who preceded them. It is they who will glitter with accomplishment."

Since I wrote that, one more star came to glitter in my life, my great-granddaughter, Alexa, born October 12, 1994. Just as Christopher Columbus discovered America on that day, so shall she discover her new world and romp through the greatest century the United States has ever seen.

The compilation of thoughts that follows has served me well during my lifetime. I decided one day to put them all in one place. It is my hope that it will also hold you in good stead.

Some of the quotations and sayings are my own, some borrowed, some stolen, but the source of the items is not material. It is their contents.

They are not listed alphabetically or in their order of importance in my life. They are all just a good bunch of sayings to live by. Look them over. Think about what these greats, near-greats, and who-is-thats? have to say. Reflect and act and you too can achieve success, happiness—and that all-important, financial independence.

One last thought as you march confidently on the road to the twenty-first century—always bear in mind that success is measured not only by how well you do, but how well you do for others.

So, read, enjoy, learn—and get out there and get something done!

LIBERTY AND FREEDOM FOR ALL

We the people of the United States, in order to form a more perfect Union, establish justice, insure domestic tranquillity, provide for the common defense, promote the general welfare, and secure the blessings of liberty to ourselves and our posterity do ordain and establish this Constitution for the United States of America.

PREAMBLE TO THE AMERICAN CONSTITUTION

That we Americans have achieved and accomplished so much in the past and have a glorious and prosperous future to look forward to in the next century is thanks to the wisdom of our founding fathers. In 1876, British statesman William Ewart Gladstone wrote in celebration of America's centennial year that "I have always regarded that Constitution as the most remarkable work known to me in modern times to have been produced by the human intellect, at a single stroke (so to speak), in its application to political affairs." That constitution has guaranteed the freedoms we enjoy. So let us begin with some thoughts on our luxury of liberty.

We hold these truths to be sacred and undeniable; that all men are created equal and independent, that from that equal creation they derive rights inherent and inalienable, among which are the preservation of life, and liberty, and the pursuit of happiness.

THOMAS JEFFERSON,
THIRD PRESIDENT OF THE UNITED STATES

This is taken from the original draft of the Declaration of Independence.

When, in the course of human events, it becomes necessary for one people to dissolve the political bands which have connected them with another, and to assume among the powers of the earth the separate and equal station to which the laws of nature and of nature's God entitle them, a decent respect to the opinions of mankind requires that they should declare the causes which impel them to the separation. We hold these truths to be self-evident; that all men are created equal; that they are endowed by their creator with certain unalienable rights; that among these are life, liberty, and the pursuit of happiness; that to secure these rights, governments are instituted among men, deriving their just powers from the consent of the governed; that whenever any form of government becomes destructive of these ends, it is the right of the people to alter or to abolish it, and to institute new government, laying its foundation on such principles, and organizing its powers in such form, as to them shall seem most likely to effect their safety and happiness.

THOMAS JEFFERSON

Liberty is the right of the individual to stand up for his rights.

Individuality is the aim of political liberty. By leaving to the citizen as much freedom of action and of being, as comports with order and the rights of others, the institutions render him truly a freeman. He is left to pursue his means of happiness in his own manner.

JAMES FENIMORE COOPER,
AMERICAN NOVELIST

Is it no wonder so many people
want to be U.S. citizens?

Democracy is not a fragile flower; still it needs cultivating.

RONALD REAGAN,
FORTIETH PRESIDENT
OF THE UNITED STATES

When it came to Ronald Reagan,
what a job he did destroying communism
and the Berlin Wall.

Long may our land be bright
With freedom's Holy Light

SAMUEL FRANCIS SMITH

And it will be, Sam Smith, with some temporary clouds and darkness as we ready for the twenty-first century.

Is life so dear or peace so sweet as to be purchased by the price of chains and slavery? Forbid it, Almighty God!

I know not what course others may take, but as for me, give me Liberty or give me death!

PATRICK HENRY,
AMERICAN PATRIOT AND ORATOR

I say, Patrick, we have held fast to your admonishment.

The proudest now is but my peer,
    The highest not more high;
Today, of all the wary year,
    A king of men am I.
Today alike are great and small,
    The nameless and the unknown,
My palace is the people's hall,
    The ballot box my throne.

JOHN GREENLEAF WHITTIER,
AMERICAN POET

I wish more of our citizens realized this and would go to the ballot box regularly.

If a nation values anything more than freedom, it will lose its freedom; and the irony of it is that if it is comfort or money that it values more, it will lose that too.

WILLIAM SOMERSET MAUGHAM,
ENGLISH NOVELIST AND PLAYWRIGHT

These are the times that try men's souls. The summer soldier and the sunshine patriot will, in this crisis, shrink from the service of their country; but he that stands it now, deserves the love and thanks of man and woman. Tyranny, like hell, is not easily conquered; yet we have this consolation with us, that the harder the conflict, the more glorious the triumph. What we obtain too cheap, we esteem too lightly; it is dearness only that gives everything its value. Heaven knows how to put a proper price upon its goods; and it would be strange indeed, if so celestial an article as Freedom should not be highly rated.

THOMAS PAINE,
AMERICAN REVOLUTIONARY AND WRITER

It is the underrating of our freedom that can be demoralizing.

Equal and exact justice to all men, of whatever state or persuasion, religious or political; peace, commerce, and honest friendship with all nations, entangling alliances with none. . . . Freedom of religion; freedom of the press, and freedom of person under the protection of the habeas corpus, and trial by juries impartially selected. These principles form the bright constellation which has gone before us, and guided our steps through an age of revolution and reformation. The wisdom of our sages and the blood of our heroes have been devoted to their attainment. They should be the creed of our political faith, the text of civil instruction, the touchstone by which to try the services of those we trust; and should we wander from them in moments of error or alarm, let us hasten to retrace our steps and to regain the road which alone leads to peace, liberty, and safety.

THOMAS JEFFERSON

Individual liberty is individual power, and as the power of a community is a mass compounded of individual powers, the nation which enjoys the most freedom must necessarily be in proportion to its numbers the most powerful nation.

JOHN QUINCY ADAMS,
SIXTH PRESIDENT OF THE UNITED STATES

And we have become the most powerful nation—
John Adams, you would be proud of us now.

Our ability to create that other freedom, the freedom of financial independence, makes our country so different from almost any other.

The ideology of capitalism makes us all into connoisseurs of liberty—of the indefinite expansion of possibility.

SUSAN SONTAG, AMERICAN ESSAYIST

Say it again, Susan.

TAKING YOUR PMA PILL: THERE REALLY IS POWER IN POSITIVE THINKING

No doubt about it, you can move mountains by approaching life with enthusiasm and a positive mental attitude. So be sure to take your PMA pill every morning (no FDA approval necessary).

There is a real magic in enthusiasm. It spells the difference between mediocrity and accomplishment.

NORMAN VINCENT PEALE,
CLERGYMAN AND AUTHOR

Morale is the state of mind. It is steadfastness and courage and hope. It is confidence and zeal and loyalty. It is élan, esprit de corps and determination.

GEN. GEORGE C. MARSHALL,
UNITED STATES ARMY

The problem when solved will be simple.

SIGN IN GENERAL MOTORS'
DAYTON RESEARCH LABORATORY

Optimism doesn't wait on facts. It deals with prospects. Pessimism is a waste of time.

NORMAN COUSINS,
EDITOR, SATURDAY REVIEW

We act as though comfort and luxury were the chief requirements of life, when all that we need to make us really happy is something to be enthusiastic about.

CHARLES KINGSLEY,
ENGLISH AUTHOR AND CLERIC

Nothing great was ever achieved without enthusiasm.

RALPH WALDO EMERSON,
AMERICAN PHILOSOPHER AND ESSAYIST

Happiness is the only good,
The time to be happy is now.
The place to be happy is here,
The way to be happy is to make others so.

BOB INGERSOLL

Ninety percent of winning is being excited.

ART WILLIAMS

My friend, Art, was so excited and enthusiastic that he helped change the map of the entire life-insurance industry.

EDUCATION: MAKING IT WORK FOR YOU

Some people have the mistaken impression that a good education automatically opens the door to success. Unfortunately, that's often not the case. What education can do is send you down the right corridor. But it's up to you to find the door and open it. And while you're looking, don't let education set up roadblocks by teaching you limitations. You hear that you can't do this. You can't do that. It can't be done. And surprise, surprise, you don't even try.

It bears repeating that you need more than theory you learn in the classroom to succeed. You need practice, practice, practice.

The ability to think straight, some knowledge of the past, some vision of the future, some skill to do useful service, some urge to fit that service into the well-being of the community—these are the most vital things education must try to produce.

VIRGINIA GILDERSLEEVE,
DEAN EMERITUS, BARNARD COLLEGE

The young man who is able to work his way through college is a pretty good bet to be able to work his way through life.

ANONYMOUS

A better truism would be hard to find.

Books are not men and
  Yet they are alive,
They are man's memory
  And his inspiration,
The link between his present
  And past,
the tools he builds with.

STEPHEN VINCENT BENÉT,
AMERICAN AUTHOR

You can bet on this one.

Our glorious land today,
  Neath education's sway,
Soar upward still.
  Its hail of learning fair.
  Whose beauties all may share,
  Behold them everywhere
On vale and hill.

SAMUEL FRANCIS SMITH,
A STANZA OF "AMERICA"

A school is not a factory. Its raison d'être is to provide opportunity for experience.

J. L. CARR, BRITISH NOVELIST.

At college age, you can tell who is best at taking tests and going to school, but you can't tell who the best people are. That worries the hell out of me.

**BARNABY C. KEENEY,
PRESIDENT, BROWN UNIVERSITY**

The basic purpose of a liberal arts education is to liberate the human being to exercise his or her potential to the fullest.

**BARBARA M. WHITE,
PRESIDENT, MILLS COLLEGE**

A student is not a professional athlete. . . . He is not a little politician or junior senator looking for angles . . . an amateur promoter, a glad-hander, embryo Rotarian, café-society leader, quiz kid or man about town. A student is a person who is learning to fulfill his powers and to find ways of using them in the service of mankind.

HAROLD TAYLOR,
PRESIDENT, SARAH LAWRENCE COLLEGE

I didn't go to high school, and I didn't go to grade school, either. Education, I think, is for refinement and is probably a liability.

H. L. HUNT, TEXAS OIL BILLIONAIRE

Much that passes for education . . . is not education at all but ritual. The fact is that we are being educated when we know it least.

DAVID P. GARDNER, PRESIDENT,
UNIVERSITY OF UTAH, SALT LAKE CITY

Nagging questions remain: Where is the line between making the most of one's potential and reaching for the unattainable? Where is the line between education as a tool and education as a kind of magic? The line is blurred and that is why when education fails, disillusionment is so bitter.

HENRY ANATOLE GRUNWALD,
EDITOR-IN-CHIEF, TIME INCORPORATED

Theory without practice is impractical.

GOALS: YOU HAVE TO MAKE THEM TO WIN THE GAME OF LIFE

You need something to aim at if you're going to hit a bullseye. Figure out what you want, and then go for it.

Most of us serve our ideals by fits and starts. The person who makes a success of living is the one who sees his goal steadily and aims for it unswervingly. That is dedication.

CECIL B. DE MILLE,
AMERICAN MOVIE DIRECTOR/PRODUCER

You should know, Mr. De Mille. Commitment to what one wants to accomplish must be steadfast.

It doesn't do any harm to dream, providing you get up and hustle when the alarm goes off.

ANONYMOUS

So do it!

Good ideas are good, good ideas are no good if not executed.

People think that at the top there isn't much room. They tend to think of it as an Everest. My message is that there is tons of room at the top.

MARGARET THATCHER,
PRIME MINISTER OF GREAT BRITAIN

It is thrifty to prepare today for the wants of tomorrow.

AESOP

The riders in a race do not stop short when they reach the goal. There is a little finishing canter before coming to a standstill. There is time to hear the kind voice of friends and to say to one's self: "The work is done." But just as one says that, the answer comes: "The race is over, but the work never is done while the power to work remains." The canter that brings you to a standstill need not be only coming to rest. It cannot be, while you still live. For to live is to function. That is all there is in living.

OLIVER WENDELL HOLMES, JR.,
AMERICAN JURIST

The tragedy of life doesn't lie in not reaching your goal. The tragedy lies in having no goal to reach.

BENJAMIN E. MAYS,
PRESIDENT, MOREHOUSE COLLEGE

I say amen!

Climb high
Climb far
Your goal the sky
Your aim the star.

ANONYMOUS

Go out and be the very best you can be.

WORKING HARD, GOING FAR, BEING HAPPY

Not long ago, a New York stockbroker died. He had worked right up to the day of his death. Unusual? Only in that he was 103. The man never considered retiring, although he certainly had the financial independence to do so. He liked to work, it gave him a sense of himself, and it made him happy.

Working hours are never long enough. Each day is a holiday, and ordinary holidays . . . are grudged as enforced interruptions in an absorbing vocation.

**WINSTON CHURCHILL,
PRIME MINISTER OF GREAT BRITAIN**

A vacation is a state of mind, and if your mind is focused, your 365-day year can be your vacation.

Far and away the best prize that life offers is the chance to work hard at work worth doing.

**THEODORE ROOSEVELT,
TWENTY-SIXTH PRESIDENT
OF THE UNITED STATES**

There is no substitute for hard work.

**THOMAS ALVA EDISON,
AMERICAN INVENTOR**

Work is much more fun than fun.

**NOEL COWARD,
ENGLISH PLAYWRIGHT, ACTOR,
DIRECTOR, COMPOSER**

The secret of joy in work is contained in one word—excellence. To know how to do something well is to enjoy it.

PEARL S. BUCK, AUTHOR

Work is honorable. Work is in the American tradition.

RUDOLPH GIULIANI,
MAYOR, CITY OF NEW YORK

Now do you understand why so many people don't like Rudy?

It is work, work that one delights in, that is the surest guarantor of happiness. But even here it is a work that has to be earned by labor in one's earlier years. One should labor so hard in youth that everything one does subsequently is easy by comparison.

ASHLEY MONTAGU, ANTHROPOLOGIST

Amen to that. Work your ass off when you're young, and you can slow down when you're older.

Storybook happiness involves every form of pleasant thumb-twiddling; true happiness involves the full use of one's powers and talents.

JOHN W. GARDNER,
PRESIDENT, CARNEGIE FOUNDATION

This is powerful.

There's always room for improvement, you know—it's the biggest room in the house.

LOUISE HEATH LEBER,
1961 MOTHER OF THE YEAR

The work of the individual still remains the spark that moves mankind ahead even more than teamwork.

IGOR SIKORSKY,
AMERICAN AERONAUTICAL ENGINEER
AND INVENTOR

Self-help must precede help from others. Even for making certain of help from heaven, one has to help oneself.

MORARJI R. DESAI,
PRIME MINISTER OF INDIA, 1977

I do not know anyone who has got to the top without hard work. That is the recipe. It will not always get you to the top, but should get you pretty near.

MARGARET THATCHER

A great prime minister with great wisdom.

The more I want to get something done, the less I call it work.

RICHARD BACH,
AUTHOR OF
JONATHAN LIVINGSTON SEAGULL

There is no time for cut-and-dried monotony. There is time for work. And time for love. That leaves no other time!

GABRIELLE "COCO" CHANEL,
FRENCH COUTURIER

The reward of a thing well done is to have done it.

RALPH WALDO EMERSON

No idleness, no laziness, no procrastination; never put off till tomorrow what you can do today.

LORD CHESTERFIELD,
ENGLISH STATESMAN AND AUTHOR

Let us, then, be up and doing,
With a heart for any fate;
Still achieving, still pursuing,
Learn to labor and to wait.

HENRY WADSWORTH LONGFELLOW,
"A PSALM OF LIFE"

Work is the grand cure for all the maladies and miseries that ever beset mankind, honest work, which you intend getting done.

THOMAS CARLYLE,
BRITISH HISTORIAN AND ESSAYIST

When work is a pleasure, life is a joy! When work is a duty, life is slavery.

MAXIM GORKY, RUSSIAN AUTHOR

I am a great believer in luck, and I find the harder I work the more I have of it.

**STEPHEN LEACOCK,
CANADIAN ECONOMIST AND HUMORIST**

Work is love made visible. And if you cannot work with love but only with distaste, it is better that you should leave your work and sit at the gate of the temple and take alms of those who work with joy.

KAHLIL GIBRAN, LEBANESE WRITER

It is not the critic who counts, not the man who points out how the strong man stumbled, or where the doer of deeds could have done them better. The credit belongs to the man who is actually in the arena; whose face is marred by dust and sweat and blood; who strives valiantly, who errs and comes short again and again; who knows the great enthusiasms, the great devotions, and spends himself in a worthy cause; who, at the best, knows in the end the triumph of high achievement; and who, at the worst, at least fails while daring greatly, so that his place shall never be with those cold and timid souls who know neither victory nor defeat.

THEODORE ROOSEVELT

EMULATING SUCCESS: IT CAN HELP YOU SUCCEED

If we study what's been done before and how, our task of becoming a success is that much easier. We not only learn from the mistakes of others, but we learn from what they did right.

What is success? I think it is a mixture of having a flair for the thing that you are doing; knowing that it is not enough, that you have got to have hard work and a certain sense of purpose.

MARGARET THATCHER

I have found that great people do have in common . . . an immense belief in themselves and in their mission. They also have great determination as well as an ability to work hard. At the crucial moment of decision, they draw on their accumulated wisdom. Above all, they have integrity.

YOUSUF KARSH, PHOTOGRAPHER

A wise man will not walk down the road of success with you. He'll simply point you in the right direction.

ANONYMOUS

A direction you will take if you are a good listener.

If a man has a talent and cannot use it, he has failed. If he has a talent and uses only half of it, he has partly failed. If he has a talent and learns somehow to use the whole of it, he has gloriously succeeded, and won a satisfaction and a triumph few men ever know.

THOMAS WOLFE, AMERICAN AUTHOR

Reason enough to do it big.

Always bear in mind that your own resolution to succeed is more important than any other one thing.

ABRAHAM LINCOLN,
SIXTEENTH PRESIDENT OF
THE UNITED STATES

Success is more a function of consistent common sense than it is of genius

AN WANG, INVENTOR,
FOUNDER OF WANG LABORATORIES

DOING UNTO OTHERS

As I've told my children and grandchildren countless times, there is more to success than what you've accomplished for yourself, the amount of money you've amassed, or the number of cars in your garage. It is also what you have done for others along the way. Doing good unto others is doing good unto yourself.

AN ADMIRABLE MAN

If a man is honest with others
    and with himself . . .
If he receives gratefully and gives quietly . . .
    If he is gentle enough to feel
and strong enough to show his feelings . . .
    If he is slow to see the faults in others
    but quick to discover their goodness . . .
If he is cheerful in difficult times
    and modest in success . . .
If he does his best to be true to his beliefs . . .
    Then he is truly an admirable man.

Money, or even power, can never yield happiness unless it be accompanied by the goodwill of others. I know a very clever businessman who is making a great deal of money, mostly by practices which are strictly legal but which have as their object outwitting, and outbargaining, not to say the hoodwinking, of others. He is less happy than almost anyone else I know.

B. C. FORBES

You don't live for yourself. You live to make life better for other people.

DR. ALBERT SABIN,
AMERICAN MICROBIOLOGIST
AND PHYSICIAN

There is an eternal law of compensation. This law was proclaimed of old in these words: "As ye sow, so shall ye reap." The wise man will choose to do his exertion while he is young, while hardship and fatigue and self-denial sit lightly on his forehead and daunt not his spirit. Every human being must put something into the world before he can hope to get all he reasonably needs out of the world—even millionaires' offspring are less exempt from this decree than we sometimes are tempted to imagine. If you begin by denying yourself nothing, the world later is apt to do your denying for you.

B. C. FORBES

The test of our progress is not
whether we add more to the abundance
of those who have much; it is whether
we have done enough for those who have too little.

FRANKLIN DELANO ROOSEVELT,
THIRTY-SECOND PRESIDENT
OF THE UNITED STATES

No act of kindness, no matter how small, is ever wasted.

AESOP

It is nice to be important, but more important to be nice.

What wisdom can you find that is greater than kindness?

**JEAN JACQUES ROUSSEAU,
FRENCH PHILOSOPHER**

I expect to pass through this world but once; any good thing therefore that I can do, or any kindness that I can show to any fellow creature, let me do it now; let me not defer or neglect it, for I shall not pass this way again.

ANONYMOUS

A good way to judge people is by observing how they treat those who can do them absolutely no good.

Do unto others as you have them do to you.

PATRIOTISM: MORE THAN "THE STAR-SPANGLED BANNER" AT THE SUPER BOWL

There's nothing wrong and everything right in loving, supporting, defending, and being proud of your country when it is as great as the United States. Patriotism is the emotional side of Americanism, and it is back in fashion—for good reason.

I believe in the United States of America as a government of the people, by the people, for the people, whose just powers are derived from the consent of the governed; a democracy in a republic; a sovereign Nation of many sovereign States; a perfect Union, one and inseparable, established upon those principles of freedom, equality, justice, and humanity for which American patriots sacrificed their lives and fortunes.

I therefore believe it is my duty to my country to love it, support its Constitution, to obey its laws, to respect its flag, and defend it against all enemies.

WILLIAM TYLER PAGE,
"AMERICAN'S CREED,"
A 1918 PRIZE-WINNING COMPOSITION

America. . . . It is a fabulous country, the only fabulous country; it is the only place where miracles not only happen, but where they happen all the time.

THOMAS WOLFE

O beautiful for spacious skies,
For amber waves of grain,
For purple mountain majesties
Above the fruited plain!
America! America!
God shed his grace on thee
And crown thy good with brotherhood
From sea to shining sea!

KATHERINE LEE BATES,
"AMERICA THE BEAUTIFUL"

One cannot be an American by going about saying that one is an American. It is necessary to feel America, like America, love America and then work.

GEORGIA O'KEEFFE,
AMERICAN ARTIST

God bless America,
Land that I love.

**IRVING BERLIN,
AMERICAN COMPOSER**

America, the land of unlimited possibilities.

**LUDWIG MAX GOLDBERGER,
AMERICAN AUTHOR**

When an American says that he loves his country, he . . . means that he loves an inner air, an inner light in which freedom lives and in which a man can draw the breath of self-respect.

**ADLAI EWING STEVENSON,
AMERICAN POLITICIAN**

O beautiful for patriot dream
That sees beyond the years.
Thine alabaster cities gleam,
Undimmed by human tears.

KATHERINE LEE BATES

When Freedom from her mountain height,
Unfurled her standard to the air,
She tore the azure robe of night,
And set the stars of glory there.

JOSEPH RODMAN DRAKE,
AUTHOR OF "THE AMERICAN FLAG"

Oh, say, can you see by the dawn's early light,
What so proudly we hailed at the twilight's last gleaming?
Whose broad stripes and bright stars, through the perilous fight,
O'er the ramparts we watched were so gallantly streaming?
And the rockets' red glare, the bombs bursting in air,
Gave proof through the night that our flag was still there.
Oh, say, does that star-spangled banner yet wave
O'er the land of the free and the home of the brave?

FRANCIS SCOTT KEY,
"THE STAR-SPANGLED BANNER"

HUDDLED MASSES YEARNING TO BREATHE FREE

They yearn to come to America so that they may breathe free, so that they may bask in our liberties, so that they may enjoy the freedom of financial independence.

None who have always been free can understand the terrible fascinating power of the hope of freedom to those who are not free.

PEARL S. BUCK

Driven from every other corner of the earth, freedom of thought and the right of private judgment in matters of conscience direct their course to this happy country as their last asylum.

SAMUEL ADAMS,
AMERICAN REVOLUTIONARY

Look! Up in the sky! It's a bird! It's a plane! It's Superman! . . . Strange visitor from another planet, who . . . fights a never-ending battle for truth, justice, and the American way.

Talk about traveling a great distance to reach the promised land.

THE AMERICAN FREE ENTERPRISE SYSTEM

It is the American free enterprise system that allows the individual to plant his or her Fortune Tree and efficiently take advantage of our country's vast resources. It's the American free enterprise system that makes the United States the envy of the rest of the world.

Agriculture, manufactures, commerce, and navigation, the four pillars of our prosperity, are then most thriving when left most free to individual enterprise. Protection from casual embarrassments, however, may sometimes be seasonably interposed.

THOMAS JEFFERSON

Next to the right of liberty, the right of property is the most important individual right guaranteed by the Constitution and the one which, united with that of personal liberty, has contributed more to the growth of civilization than any other institution established by the human race.

WILLIAM HOWARD TAFT,
TWENTY-SEVENTH PRESIDENT
OF THE UNITED STATES

Freedom in economic arrangements is itself a component of freedom broadly understood, so economic freedom is an end in itself. . . . Economic freedom is also an indispensable means toward the achievement of political freedom.

**MILTON FRIEDMAN,
AMERICAN ECONOMIST**

Market competition is the only form of organization which can afford a large measure of freedom to the individual.

FRANK HYNEMAN KNIGHT

MOVING INTO THE FUTURE: ALL YOU NEED IS THE RIGHT ADDRESS

To all the young people in the United States, I say the future is bright, the future is yours. Great growth and prosperity are awaiting you, as long as you stride into the next century with confidence, a plan for success, and tremendous enthusiasm.

This generation of Americans has a rendezvous with destiny.

FRANKLIN DELANO ROOSEVELT, IN A 1936 SPEECH

The same applies to this generation, even more so.

Hats off to the past, coats off to the future.

ANONYMOUS

The only limitations to our realization of tomorrow is the limitation which we, by our lack of faith, limited vision, and doubt of the future, impose today.

ELLIS ARNALL, GOVERNOR OF GEORGIA

The empires of the future are the empires of the mind.

WINSTON CHURCHILL

With our eyes fixed on the future, but recognizing the realities of today . . . we will achieve our destiny to be as a shining city on a hill for all mankind to see.

RONALD REAGAN

It's morning again in America.

SLOGAN FOR RONALD REAGAN'S ELECTION CAMPAIGN

Neither a wise man nor a brave man lies down on the tracks of history to wait for the train of the future to run over him.

DWIGHT D. EISENHOWER, THIRTY-FOURTH PRESIDENT OF THE UNITED STATES

The one with the primary responsibility to the individual's future is that individual.

DORCAS HARDY,
DIRECTOR, SOCIAL SECURITY SYSTEM

I say amen and amen, again. It was the intent of FDR in 1937 to develop a social security system that was simply a floor for financial protection. Then it was up to each individual to build a house above the floor.

We make our future by the best use of the present.

Consumers are more knowledgeable, aggressive in their thoughts and grossly inquisitive about their future than they ever used to be.

I have but one lamp by which my feet are guided, and that is the lamp of experience. I know of no way of judging the future but by the past.

PATRICK HENRY

If you do not think about the future, you cannot have one.

JOHN GALSWORTHY,
NOBEL PRIZE-WINNING BRITISH AUTHOR

The illusion that time that were are better than those that are has probably pervaded all ages.

HORACE GREELEY,
AMERICAN JOURNALIST AND POLITICIAN

RANDOM THOUGHTS WORTH THINKING

As to your friends and associates, when in doubt, leave them out.

The patient investor gets compounded. The impatient investor gets confounded.

Everyone must take charge of his own life. Drugs destroy hopes and opportunity.

You cannot do anything about the length of your life, but you can do something about its width and depth.

It ain't over till it's over.

YOGI BERRA, BASEBALL GREAT

Give to the world the best you have
And the best will come back to you.

CATHARINE WRIGHT,
MY FORMER HOUSEKEEPER

Your prescription for personal growth in our growing country should involve second and third opinions.

Money matters—and you better believe it!

The people and their overindulgence in plastic card spending have caused much financial indigestion, leading to physical and mental illness and actually adding to the divorce and suicide rates.

We now live in a world of deflation, and it will affect everybody. It is no longer possible to pass on increased costs from bad management and nonproductivity to the consumer. The old cliché "Let the Buyer Beware" has been changed by educated consumers; it is now "Let the Competition Beware."

Assume nothing, supervise everything.

When I have to do any selling—and all of us are salesmen in one sense or another—I try to say, not as much as possible, but as little as is necessary to get the other man talking, and then I encourage him to say whatever is on his mind. Almost everybody likes to talk. Nobody likes to be talked at. Let your prospect have the floor. Say just enough to arouse his interest and get him to ask questions. Your job is to tell him what he wants to know, not bore him with a stereotyped patter-patter of words which are ground out as if from a hurdy-gurdy organ, so metallic do they ring.

B. C. FORBES

More business deals and sales are not made because we lack the understanding to be good listeners.

A thing of beauty is a joy forever,
Its loveliness increases,
It will never pass into nothingness.

JOHN KEATS, ENGLISH POET

[Daddy] said: "All children must look after their own upbringing." Parents can only give good advice or put them on the right paths, but the final forming of a person's character lies in their own hands.

ANNE FRANK,
JEWISH DIARIST AND HOLOCAUST VICTIM

It matters not if you lose or win, it's how you play the game that counts.

He who speaks the loudest is the least heard.

The trouble with most folks isn't so much their ignorance as knowing so many things that ain't so.

Money can't buy class.

Patience is a virtue.

If each of us can be helped by science to live a hundred years, what will it profit us if our hates and fears, our loneliness and our remorse will not permit us to enjoy them? What use is an extra year or two to the man who "kills" what time he has.

DAVID NEISWANGER,
MENNINGER FOUNDATION

Sometime ago you were so kind
A book you loaned me that was not mine.
From it I studied and learned
And so it is here to be returned.

(I hope you won't lend this book to too many of your friends. Their initiative in going to the library or bookstore can be their first effort to their success.)